Rivers

ABRAMS/MERIDIAN MODERN ARTISTS

Sam Hunter

Rivers

Harry N. Abrams book for Meridian Books

The Abrams/Meridian Modern Artists Series is published by
Harry N. Abrams, Inc., and distributed by
The World Publishing Company, New York
Standard Book Number: 8109-2104-9
Library of Congress Catalogue Card Number: 71-175945
Printed in Japan

Contents

List of Plates

Colorplates are marked with an asterisk*

Rivers

ABRAMS/MERIDIAN MODERN ARTISTS

LARRY RIVERS POSSESSES A NATURAL AND GENEROUS TALENT for providing journalists with "copy" by his actions in and out of art, but his theatrical verve in recent years, unfortunately, threatened to distract serious attention from his very considerable artistic achievement. Too often he has been taken as an engaging public performer, and some of his critics make the mistake of confusing his irrepressible exhibitionism with an imagined artistic flaw of fitful or unsteady inspiration. Then there is Rivers' association with artistic scandal, beginning with his historic *Washington Crossing the Delaware*, a painting which outraged avant-garde sensibilities in the early fifties. This large work is now considered a proto-Pop masterpiece with its place in modern American art history assured. In its time, however, the remake of a famous pictorial cliché after Emmanuel Leutze was viewed as a betrayal of principle by the Action painters to whom Rivers professed allegiance.

When a series of unflattering nude "academies" followed in Rivers' art, he was castigated even more severely as an incorrigible rebel and figure of controversy who presumed to defy the reigning abstract artists. He did not help his reputation among the more priggish members of the progressive art establishment by his appearance on a television quiz program, where he matched wits and art expertise with a jockey and a minor movie star. Rivers' frequent eruptions into print with uninhibited declarations on art and life, his history as a jazz musician, and his extravagant dress and immense personal vitality have, in conjunction with a resounding artistic success, made him something of a celebrity. The tendency, under the circumstances, is for commentators to emphasize the public entertainer and to take the private artist and his work with something less than a full measure of seriousness.

Around New York and Southampton, where he lives in winters and summers respectively, Rivers is immediately

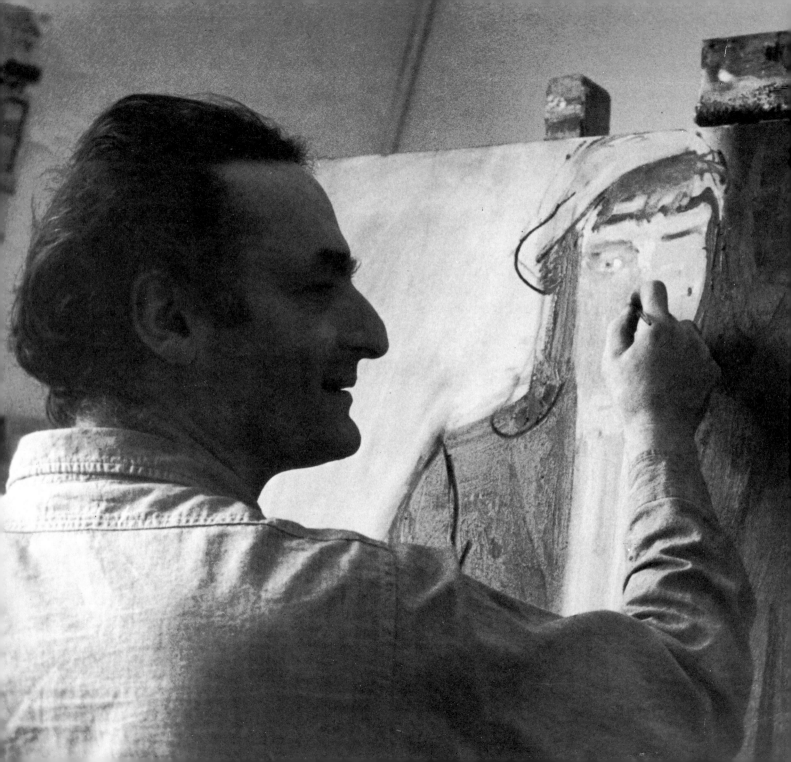

identified by his flamboyant attire—cowpuncher's boots, elaborately decorated shirts, gaudy hand painted neckties. He is also known for his addiction to imported cars, motorcycles, and jazz. He was a professional jazz musician before he embarked on a full-time career in art, and he still frequently blows the saxophone with friends from the world of entertainment, for pleasure and relaxation. His mobile, expressive face and abrupt gestures are as unforgettable as his colorful dress, and as astonishing as his many-sided involvements in art and life. He is a natural "ham," capable of registering a wide range of emotion with a comical exaggeration of mien and gesture, like some old-time tragedian from the Yiddish theater. Rivers has been a familiar and accessible figure in the New York art world for more than fifteen years, haunting its shifting sequence of favored bars, salvaging dull or muddleheaded art symposiums by his clarity, outspoken candor, and picturesque turns of speech, generously throwing open his Southampton summer house to an endless troop of artists, poets, students, collectors, petitioners, and curiosity-seekers with only the vaguest credentials; many come only to listen and admire, to be able to report that they met "the fantastic Larry Rivers."

Within the New York art world, Rivers fashioned a new and potent artistic identity which mixed hedonism with disciplined craft, the existentialist self-reference of the Action painters and a more lighthearted autobiographical obsession. Ingeniously, he made art of his own life, his friends, his family, and perversely, even from a nostalgic dream of art history and lofty "tradition." His art, in fact, thrived magnificently on the very contradictions so conspicuously advertised by his life.

In painting, Rivers' first and in many ways still his most radical achievement was the historic *Washington Crossing the Delaware*, an effort of mixed sincerity and ironic inspiration to create a Salon "machine." It was an impressionistic improvisation after Emmanuel Leutze's patriotic celebration in paint, which every American schoolboy knows by heart. In its own time, the Rivers' painting was received as a visual polemic, a reaction he encouraged by repeated statements disassociating himself from abstract art; in retrospect, the painting is most appealing as a prophesy of Pop Art's interest in American folklore and the commonplace. It offered viable alternatives to Action Painting long before the New Realists and Pop artists.

No one at the time foresaw that Rivers' counterrevolution in style and subject matter might lead to the Pop Art of the sixties. What then must have seemed an exercise in nostalgia was later to be understood, more complexly and equivocally, to contain distinct elements of conscious irony and parody. The fact that Rivers refused to distinguish between "good" art and "bad," between the vulgarity of Leutze's Washington and the artistic refinement of Géricault's *Nude Study*, two sources of his early work, was itself significant and anticipated the more democratic and matter-of-fact attitudes of a later generation. As the pendulum of art swung away from invention and the subjective idealism of the Abstract Expressionists, the "inspiring" and hierarchic subject gave way to popular sources in the search for new imagery.

Rivers continued to challenge contemporary taste, even as he seemed to follow furtively the dictates of his retrospective mood, in his justly acclaimed "allegories" of the mid-fifties. His art energetically fused blurred and fragmented human figures and disembodied decorative motifs of great vivacity—a mode of "spotty sensuousness," in Harold Rosenberg's apt phrase—extracted from his own life and surroundings. A number of these paintings, climaxed by *The Studio* of 1956, were of monumental scale and striking originality, memorable in the American art of the postwar period. The new mode made a virtue of a style of visual digression, but his spirited pictorial journalism, tossed off, it seemed, with mindless ease and facility, also managed to take on the power of personal myth. His favorite models—his mother-in-law, "Berdie," and the late poet, Frank O'Hara, among others—became somehow representative and enduring embodiments of a fresh and compelling artistic vision, especially in the series of extraordinary, large figure compositions of 1956.

Then, with the growing prestige of the New Realism of Rauschenberg and Johns in 1957, Rivers increasingly made the insignia of standard brands and commercial products his subject, wherever he found them relevant to his painterly sensibility. There was always an impeccable internal logic at work in the changes of his art, whatever their apparent external stimulation. The evolution of his modified Pop themes depends, in fact, as much on his own early work as on the ambience of the sixties, which they helped create and influence.

Then he abruptly turned his back on the lyricism of style that had won him public adulation, in favor of more challenging alternatives. He has recently shown a new and marked versatility in untried materials—wood, scrap metal, shaped canvas, plastic, plaster molds—and such unfamiliar techniques as mechanical silkscreening and large-scale carpentry. He achieved roughhewn, inelegant, and even amateurish effects of surface quite uncharacteristic in their "brutalism." One did not immediately recognize the seductive Rivers "touch," or his great natural fluency as a draftsman. Both his large, deliberated compositions, and his intimate small sketches—particularly the swiftly drawn portraits of friends and familiar public figures of international Bohemia—had established him as the most gifted representational draftsman and portraitist of his generation. In the past decade he seemed indifferent to that reputation, as he embarked on a more difficult course, trying altogether more primitive expressive effects.

He took up a wide variety of old and new themes, from standard brands to modern intellectual history—from the Dutch Masters' cigar icon to the Russian Revolution—and developed them side by side in the contrasting mediums of drawing, painting, mechanical printing, and three-dimensional construction. With great resourcefulness, he has managed to assimilate into his art untried techniques, a coarser surface and texture, and a new literalism of approach in the form of object impedimenta ranging from raw wood to aluminum storm windows. His inspired, if makeshift, carpentry and multifarious materials were absorbed as choice morsels of felicitous handling, with that unerring sensuousness which never seems to abandon him no matter how rapidly or wildly his stylistic direction may fluctuate. Stimulated by the new technologies of image-making and by the "environmental" expansiveness of Pop Art, he felt challenged in 1965 to attempt a new kind of visual narrative on a monster scale, the thirty-three-foot long mural, *The History of the Russian Revolution: From Marx to Mayakovsky*. This elaborate painting-construction richly summarized his artistic styles and ideological and artistic preoccupation with history and heroes.

Curiously, *The Russian Revolution* fell flat among the new vanguard where Rivers' kind of freewheeling individualism no longer carries much weight, since the focus of art is elsewhere. One can only surmise—for it was greeted with severe silence, generally—that the handmade, patchy, assemblage must have seemed as anachronistic to the new "cool" generation as the breadth of its intellectual sympathies appeared self-indulgent or sentimental. Rivers' expressive anarchism in freely mixed modes of handling, his intellectual content and explicitness of theme, his unremitting spirit of improvisation on the grand scale, and perhaps just simply his messiness—all these qualities were alien to the impersonal, rigid temper of both the Pop artists and the immaculate new abstractionists. An expressionist and ego-centered art has lost its meaning for the younger artists, who manage to polarize the most influential aesthetic viewpoints today into two opposing positions.

Larry Rivers came to painting almost accidentally, after a promising start on another career, as a jazz musician. In 1943, at the age of twenty, he was discharged from the army with a medical disability, and he began to earn his living by playing the saxophone with Shep Fields, Jerry Wald, and other "name" bands. His interest in painting was awakened by the first of a series of chance personal encounters, at least by his own reckoning. The decisive moments in his life and art seem to have occurred fortuitously—when he recounts his personal history—as if fate and accident were magically interwoven. We soon learn, however, that such miraculous changes in direction were anticipated in advance and were, in fact, chosen. They conveniently fit a master plan of self-development that had been waiting to be set in motion. Thus, in the summer of 1945, Rivers met a fellow jazz musician's wife, Jane Freilicher, the artist who first encouraged him to paint. She also introduced him to the sophisticated modes of twentieth-century art in the form, appropriate for a musician, of Braque's Cubist improvisation, *Homage to J. S. Bach*. That summer he began to paint in earnest, and later he set himself up in a modest New York studio, painting during the day and playing the saxophone at night.

Nell Blaine, a Village neighbor, further advanced his burgeoning art career and deepened his commitment to painting as a full-time vocation. She was the first established painter he met in New York, a former student of Hans Hofmann whose work was, significantly, realistic, although based on the pictorial dynamics of the Hofmann school method. She urged Rivers to enroll at Hofmann's, and he did so in January of 1947. He studied with Hofmann continuously in New York and Provincetown through the summer of 1948. Then he began attending classes at New York University, where he painted under William Baziotes and other New York School luminaries, with the idea of ultimately using art teaching rather than jazz to support himself. He earned his degree in 1951, and although he has on occasion given art instruction, he has never been forced to teach regularly to subsist.

Rivers held his first one-man show in 1949 at the Jane Street Gallery; a number of his paintings were free copies after Bonnard, and all showed his direct influence. Derivative though the exhibition was, it called forth special praise and encouragement from the critic Clement Greenberg, who called Rivers an "amazing beginner." The following year Greenberg and Meyer Schapiro selected him for the Kootz Gallery's "New Talent 1950" show, and with that exhibition his career was auspiciously launched. Singled out by two of the leading champions of American vanguard art, he found himself at the forefront of the new generation with a reputation to uphold and maintain. In the following year the major expectations his talent had aroused were confirmed, it seemed, with the completion of his first ambitious large composition, *The Burial*. The painting was later purchased, on the advice of Meyer Schapiro, for the Gloria Vanderbilt foundation and given to the Fort Wayne Art School and Museum. In *The Burial*, Rivers achieved his first sustained expression in a personal idiom, and also showed himself capable of a major effort of some scope.

2. Mrs. Bertha ("Berdie") Burger,
the artist's mother-in-law, Southampton, 1953.
Photo by Rudolph Burckhardt

The tonalities are rather somber in the shaggy, loosely brushed composition of figures huddled around a bier in the open air, but there are crude, thick slashes of glistening green and blue pigment of a vernal freshness. It was this quality that led De Kooning to liken Rivers' work "to burying your head in the grass" a short time later, when a New York magazine asked leading Abstract Expressionists to select younger artists whose work seemed most promising. To be generously praised by one of his culture heroes was immensely flattering to Rivers, and although *The Burial* was figurative and an impression of a scene, it showed the influence of De Kooning's swiftly moving brush and color rhythms. In scale, this large painting may be read as a challenge to the vast Abstract Expressionist canvases of the period, but perhaps even more striking was its open association with tradition, for the file of dark silhouettes is recognizably derived from Courbet's *A Burial at Ornans*. The painting was inspired, more personally, by the memory of his grandmother's funeral, which was recalled in vivid images in his private journal and apparently left on him a profound impression. The draped bier and the partially eradicated facial masks, as well as the theme of elegy, were revived many years later in the *Last Civil War Veteran* series; his immediate family and more distant relations, mediated by the photograph album, were also to form an important part of the iconography of his art.

Shortly after, Rivers found the beginnings of a consistent and mature personal style in the first of a series of studies of his mother-in-law, Berdie, and the innumerable preparatory pencil and small oil sketches that preceded it. After a period of personal crisis and illness in 1953, he had taken a house in Southampton with his mother-in-law, Mrs. Bertha Burger, and his two young sons, Joseph and Steven. There he found himself in a new style of painting. He had worked briefly in 1952 experimenting with rough abstract collages of great material density, and he then did some rather wildly expressionist figure drawings and paintings close in style to De Kooning's *Woman*. Neither manner satisfied him or persisted. A series of drawings leading up to *Portrait of Berdie* was critical to his technical evolution, and that completed painting brought drawing and color together in the fluent harmony that established the rudiments of his characteristic style. His palette lightened, and so did the pressures of his hand. Paint was applied in thin transparent washes rather than thick and opaque strokes, allowing him to find his image more swiftly and still characterize his subject in essential outline. Out of a welter of sensitive scribbles and color zones, he built an emergent kind of image with a blurry human recognizability—the sum of accident, erasures, gestural marks, and alternately description and disembodied contours, like so much of Action Painting.

With an astonishing virtuosity, Rivers tried his hand, beginning in 1951, at a number of life-size figurative sculptures; in mixtures of plaster and cement he discovered massive equivalents for the balance of stolid description and amorphous surface definition which characterized his new manner of drawing in paint. The plastery whiteness of his forms, their somewhat illegible edges, and the existential truthfulness of aspect of these fascinating sculptures give them an uncanny relationship in presence and surface to George Segal's plaster shells cast from live models in the sixties. Rivers' figures were created singly, and the contemporary environment, or a relationship to other figures through a shared scene or activity, was absent. His figures are not characters, or representations in a slice-of-life, theatrically heightened situation, like Segal's gas-station attendants, bus riders, lovers embracing in a real apartment hallway, or similar genres. Their drama is more one of combining a startling naturalness with vagrant memories and stylistic echoes

of Rodin, of Degas, and of Picasso's *Shepherd with Lamb*. The forms are haunting, especially with the hindsight of the sixties, because, rough and unfinished though they are, they suggest a confusion of identity; they are funerary sculptures, life-size duplicates of real human beings, more actual than artistic, even if they are missing a suitable environmental stage as a frame for action.

Rivers' *Portrait of Berdie* and his unusual sculptures seemed to enjoy general approbation. His evolution of a personal style that mixed spontaneous effects of surface and realistic observation was being followed by his peers with interest and sympathy. A more controversial reception greeted the large project begun shortly after the Berdie portrait was completed, *Washington Crossing the Delaware*. That ambitious work brought to a dramatic climax the new drift in the younger generation towards recognizable subject matter, and stirred a heated debate. De Kooning's *Woman* series and the abortive return of a fragmentary figuration in Pollock's painting had given sanction to figurative expression within the current and dominating abstract modes. Rivers, however, had taken the unexpected step of making a deliberate "history" painting, inspired by Emmanuel Leutze's academic "machine," and by American folklore. Sentiment and nostalgia, a deliberate "corniness" of content, were considered inadmissible among vanguard artists; the painstaking manner in which Rivers deliberately built up his theme from a series of drawings of individual figures and groups seemed pedantic and secondhand. It called into question the whole cult of spontaneity, and the accidentalism of Abstract Expressionism.

By taking an outworn myth from our national folklore, Rivers had opened up new sources for art in banal themes and visual commonplaces. The triteness of his subject broke down the hierarchical distinctions between what was and was not appropriate to "advanced" American art. The theme he selected appealed to Rivers' taste for action, history, and heroism, but also to his sense of irony. By reviving a despicable visual cliché—which even he himself made no pretense of literally re-creating or putting much credence in—he raised questions about the content of contemporary art.

The work was inspired by his reading of Tolstoy's *War and Peace*. He began to work on the war panorama by sketching, in the Southampton library, from crude children's book illustrations of Revolutionary soldiers and settled finally on Leutze's popular academic composition as his main iconographic source. There are unexpected juxtapositions in the painting of imagery derived from popular illustration and from the old masters; one of the many expressive drawings preceding the painting of Washington's visage was a free copy of the face of the fiercely grimacing, equestrian figure in Rubens' drawing after the famous Leonardo cartoon, *The Battle of Anghiari*. Rivers seemed to proceed by the simplest associations on the theme of war and culled his allusions and models from whatever illustrated precedents lay ready at hand. His impartial reliance on such mixed sources coupled with his enjoyment of the contradiction between "high" and vernacular art sources was one of the most original features of the large and impressive work. Sometime later in an interview, he told James Thrall Soby: "I kept wanting to make a picture out of a national myth, to accept the 'impossible' and the 'corny' as a challenge instead of running away. . . . I guess I wanted to paint something in the tradition of the Salon picture, which modern artists hold in contempt. Besides, there was plenty in 'Washington Crossing the Delaware' to dazzle me—horses, water, soldiers, and so on."

The following year continued the controversy over Rivers' intentions when he painted a number of "academies" of his family and friends posed nude, in a harsh and uncompromisingly naturalistic manner. There is a searching honesty in these somewhat clumsy but affecting works, as if the artist felt almost too desperately that his artistic credentials depended on identifying himself with the grand manner. And his subjects are a curious mixture of dignity and vulnerability. *Augusta* and *O'Hara* are two seven-foot-high nude studies of exceptional candor in which Rivers used his first wife and the poet Frank O'Hara as models. The paintings evoke the artificial atmosphere of the nineteenth-century salon, and Rivers seems determined to embrace uncritically the least attractive features of academic art: stiff rhetorical pose and murky tonalities. The fact that a Delacroix study was the source of *Augusta*, and a newly acquired Géricault, at the Metropolitan Museum of Art, of *O'Hara*, made his break with abstraction even more explicit. Yet his eye was unerring and of instinctive honesty; the definition of his human forms has a fragile and touchingly thin-limbed, awkward grace. They are drab, but still poetic figures rendered in a limping, strangely anachronistic style. Rivers' odyssey of self-discovery, as he tried out the postures and expressive conventions of the official salon, was perhaps the main point of these inventions.

In *The Family* Rivers posed his two undressed young sons with their fully clothed grandmother, in an obvious reference to Manet's *Déjeuner sur L'Herbe*. Like Manet, he enjoyed the contrast of textures of exposed flesh and clothed figures, and the complications of decorative motifs in the unfinished background. Another painting that brought notoriety, *Bedroom*, shows a married couple starkly nude, but their clear, unembarrassed regard and the increasingly deft, decorative pictorial accessories divert the eye from any prurient interest. It is Rivers' respect for his own experience,

4. *O'Hara*. 1954.
   Oil on canvas, 97 × 53".
   Collection the artist

5. Théodore Géricault. *A Nude Study.*
Oil on canvas, 31 3/4 × 25 3/8".
The Metropolitan Museum of Art, New York.
Rogers Fund, 1952

including an elementary candor about sex and gender, that emerges in these works, rather than scandalous intention. And there is another quality which makes itself strongly felt: his mind's capacity for visual *non sequiturs* and significant distraction, psychologically so much like our perception of life itself.

Rivers' mood of harsh naturalism culminated in his extraordinary *Double Portrait of Berdie*, a painting that drew perhaps more fire from artists and critics than *Washington Crossing the Delaware*. It seemed an even more outrageous attack on avant-garde positions, both for its retrograde realist style, and for its cruelly exact registration of flawed and aging flesh. The fact that the artist had posed his own mother-in-law in the nude struck some as perverse, a way of humiliating his subject by making a public exhibition of her naked body. Like much of Rivers' art, the painting did seem to have a diaristic element, and that tended to make the observer uneasy. In a long review in *Arts*, the critic Leo Steinberg railed against the painting's technical ineptitudes and then summarized it as "a picture in which genuine nastiness couples with false charm."

Viewed across the span of seventeen years, the painting seems technically clumsy and even barbarous. What are we to make of the arbitrary shadows that eat away the back of the seated figure, the oversize, clumsy feet and hands, and the unsure articulation of anatomy? Limbs, head, shoulders are misaligned rather than organically connected or convincing. The work seems to have evolved in fits and starts, as if seen through an erratically moving magnifying glass that inconsequently paused over certain areas of the human form and cavalierly ignored others. Of pivotal and compensating interest today is the painting's psychology of representation. By showing Berdie twice, Rivers presented the first artistic evidence of a preference for standardized and repeating images, a concern with the problem of illusionism and representation rather than the painting act itself or the springs and energies of action in the human figure. The double images of Berdie are treated with a curious lack of passion as things among other things, on the level of the furniture and decorative accessories. The repetition of image undercut the position of the Action painters that uniqueness was indispensable to expression.

Rivers' illusionism was never again to be quite so unrelenting and severe. His portrait of *Berdie in the Garden* is the first of a number of softened, more lyrical characterizations of his family and friends. In the middle fifties Rivers gained a deserved reputation as America's most gifted young portraitist, one of the rare artists who combined interest in the human personality with an authentic personal style. His feat in portraiture was to make a flesh tone or a defining edge do double duty as evocative description and design. *Joseph*, a portrait of his elder son, fuses the figure with a setting of a disorderly room with art books spilling from a bookcase, drawings tacked to the wall, and a lamp close-up that frames the scene. Such inanimate props and references to his own life and studio interests, as they were repeated, began to take on the character of myth, a convention of place and time identifying his personal world and artistic vocation.

The climactic paintings of 1956, *The Journey*, *The Athlete's Dream*, and *The Studio*, collect a familiar personae of family and friends in multiple exposure, but their large scale and generalization of image elevate Rivers' intimate world to the level and intensity of fable. An increasing element of fantasy is noticeable in the clownish, circus poses and bizarre costume of *The Athlete's Dream* and *The Journey*. Polka dots, sailor-shirt stripes, and bright flowered patterns move freely in space, liberated from the needs of local definition; the poses of the figures are relaxed, wry, and even comical, departing from their familiar grooves towards a kind of caricature of themselves. Figure contour, facial expression, stance, and gesture appear and disappear in zones of blurred, thin color, write themselves in the air, and come to a halt in a cluster of brushstrokes, or a flourish of calligraphy. Despite the exaggeration of pose and outrageous garb, the anomalous troupe manages to stand for something representative and enduring in the artist's experience.

The Studio was Rivers' most ambitious and considered venture since *Washington Crossing the Delaware*, a "realistic" allegory of his own life inviting comparison to Courbet's summary of his position in history and among his contemporaries in his famous painting also called *The Studio*. Berdie is seated at the far right in double exposure, the artist's son Joseph is positioned to the immediate right of a pot-bellied stove, his other son, Steven, is seen nude in three different positions, and Frank O'Hara stands with his foot on a scale, farthest to the left. The studio interior, foliage, and house fronts from the landscape mysteriously intermingle. The human figures are ranged across the surface in frontal poses, and in a flat friezelike sequence and rhythm. They seem to stand, each in his own private world, connected and related by their blurred and repeated definition, and by the circulating rhythm of a kind of daisy-chain arabesque of free-floating decorative motifs. The pivot of the composition is a fully realized Negro girl, her dark, warm flesh beautifully painted, bearing aloft the faint outlines of a banner on which is just discernible the half-erased legend, "Liberty"; *Art News* very appropriately dubbed her the "Muse of Liberality." The checked patterns of Berdie's dress and bits of the design break loose and float freely in space, caught up in a subtle rhythmic flow and forming points of spatial stress and articulation. A sense of pictorial space as a created continuum, given life by the artist's brush under his developing hand, has been brought into a refined equilibrium with realistic observation; the artist's life and milieu open themselves out before the eye like an unfurled scroll.

Nothing in Rivers' work before 1960 looks more contemporary today than *The Accident*, which presents a fresh view of the agitated mosaic of urban life. The episodic and filmic action revolves around successive scenes of an auto accident on the New York streets: an injured victim is helped onto a stretcher and placed in an ambulance, detectives take notes, the life of the city goes on. Competitive with the depicted action are an intruding, lively jumble of realistic references to locale, printed legends in diminutive scale—the detail of a Hershey bar, detached from the side of a truck, the lettering "real" with the word estate obliterated—numbers, abstract signs in bright confetti colors, and fully inflected paint passages in juicy impasto. The colliding realities of art and life coexist: an overturned vehicle sends up a spray of vaporous paint marks, a series of repeated circles become the wheels and movement of a car. The action of life and the medium of paint constantly interchange and displace each other.

Perhaps sensing a growing diffuseness in his art and too great a graphic emphasis, in 1958 and 1959 Rivers for the first time began to take on the unequivocal look of an Action painter. He enlarged and simplified his images and came under the influence of Franz Kline, flooding his surfaces with large homogeneous areas of dark tone. The new turn in style was to culminate a few years later in the painterly fullness and broad elisions of *Buick Painting with P* and *Ford Truck Painting*, works that state their message in simple, powerful movements of paint, without recourse to the customary linear intricacy.

The new breadth and simplification of manner were combined with a renewed interest in commonplace subject matter, alternating between the reproduced reality of the photograph and visual emblems of standard commercial brands. *Drugstore* is the first of a series of theme and variations based on a photograph of the artist standing with a girl in a print dress before a pharmacy window which advertises Dr. West's "Miracle Tuft" toothbrush. The photograph, both as an intimate source of personal history and as a ready-made reduction of reality, had attracted Rivers as early as 1956 in the painting he made of a family group, *Europe II*. Another work based on photographs, *Me II*, is a large, ambitious venture in painted autobiography, composed of small, scattered vignettes of family life from babyhood to full maturity. First, family snapshots and then special aspects of illustrated journalism offered Rivers a sense of continuity with the movement of life, while putting the necessary distance between him and events. In *Drugstore*, and in subsequent themes taken from reproduced magazine photographs, he found a flatter, more iconic compositional form, without surrendering the quality of human sentiment that continued to attract him.

Two *Life* magazine photographs of the last surviving Civil War veteran, alive and lying in state, provided the kind of nostalgic and ceremonial occasion that engaged his human sympathies and stimulated pictorial invention. The manner of handling is not interpretive and suggests neither melancholy nor regret, but the choice of episode is significant. Three large painted variations are based on the photograph of the ancient and feeble veteran among the living; two show his corpse laid out among his military relics and honors, and there are a number of wonderfully vivid small oil sketches on each theme. One large painting, *Dying and Dead Veteran*, combines aspects of both reproduced photographs. Their dualities include the sense of historical and present time, mass circulation imagery—with its anonymous registration of events in the context of a personally inflected oil painting—and, of course, the two aspects of the human form, living and dead. In all versions the flag emblem is dominant and largely edits out the human presence, expanding to fill the flat surface of the painting; the surface itself is materially rich in pigment substance, a dazzling exhibition of Rivers' painterly powers and control.

In his paintings after 1956 Rivers hinted repeatedly in a teasing now-you-see-it, now-you-don't manner at the increasing viability for art of signs and references to the commonplace. However, these allusions to a "vulgar" subject matter remained marginal to his main interest—a digressive undercurrent and mild disclaimer to the canonic painterly styles of the Abstract Expressionists. In an unexpected shift of context within an essentially impressionistic record of the artist's studio interior, *Second Avenue with "THE"*, there appears the word "THE"; it is actually the fragment of a street sign seen through his studio window. About the same time Jasper Johns made the word "the" the subject of a painting. Both are early examples, independent of each other and apparently coincidental, of fastening on an "uninteresting" subject. The ensign in *Berdie with the American Flag* occupies more of available pictorial space and consequently absorbs more of our attention. Rivers' quirky "smorgasbord of the recognizable" was threatening to take center stage and become a dominating pictorial strategy.

In 1957 and 1958, such abrupt shifts in subject seemed motivated still by the enjoyment of a banal *non sequitur* for its own sake, for its power to divert and release the eye from the main content of painterly invention. Then in 1959 there was a significant change in emphasis; the stereotype was enlarged, underscored, made palpable. It took decisive control of the painting surface. Two variations on the *Cedar Bar Menu*, in 1959 and 1960, identify the whole painting rectangle with the motif of a bill of fare. Instead of being in the painting, the motif becomes the painting, expanding to fill the surface from edge to edge. This was the kind of visual ambiguity which Jasper Johns was concurrently exploiting so brilliantly by transposing the American flag into a complete painting field.

When Rivers embarked in the early sixties on explicit Pop Art themes taken from photographs and the products of the mass media, he showed consistent if not immediately conscious preferences of subject in terms of his preoccupations of the past and his technical gifts. He was drawn to the Dutch Masters' cigar-box label because it in turn reproduced Rembrandt's *Syndics*, and gave him the opportunity to modulate a theme both in crude and more finished definition across popular media and back to its original source in fine art. The medium of traditional art is the theme of his popular subjects; the contemporary world, the object of his "fine arts" handling and painterly virtuosity. His Webster cigar-box covers oppress the eye with their trite and primitivistic human icons, but their garlanded borders invite the artist's free brush to operate expansively.

A liquid-eyed Napoleon, taken from the French hundred-franc note in the *French Money* series, reincarnated Rivers' theatrical hero image, and the baroque ornament of the scrolled and foliated setting appealed to the fabulist side of his talent. Other references also explain themselves in terms of the bias of his eye and sensibility: the ancient heraldic device of the modern playing card face whose linear convolutions he enjoyed, the Dreyfus Fund lions stalking the street with a Surrealist incongruity but mounting pedestals to imitate heroic public monuments. These images are cultivated as painterly occasions, but they allude to explicit popular sources. Sometimes, the art process itself is their subject. The emblems of lyre and torch sconces of the French franc note are reduced to patches of pure pigment, suggesting the palette's elements in their rudimentary state—i.e., their identity as notes for a project enclosed within the finished work but holding themselves aloof from the image which is their issue.

Increasingly, Rivers' versatility and experimentalism in a variety of materials and mediums have become more marked. In the face of the overwhelming transformations of art today, his work has fallen prey in influence to the changes it helped effect. Contrarily, the invasion of high art by the elementary modes of visualization and the pasteboard, emblematic reality of Pop culture, also impelled him to preserve, with added insistence, his own particular brand of individualism. He has assimilated Pop Art components of slick plastic, mechanically transferred images, machine lettering and stenciled labels, and object appendages as a harmonious scheme of painterly effects.

The jumbled lettering and jerry-built images of a 1956 exhibition announcement can be viewed as a primitive and activist form of Pop, an advertisement for himself in poster form that is also freely drawn. The inciting collage-message of his *Window Webster* makes vivid colored papers function as paint, and in *Lions on the Dreyfus Fund IV* paint is lifted, scumbled, and smeared to imitate paper cutouts and foreign material textures. The process culminated in his immense *First New York Film Festival Billboard* for Lincoln Center in 1963, with its curious reversals and ambiguities. It was a billboard announcing an actual event, designed to be seen from the street but resolutely painted by hand. The compositional style actually imitates billboard presentation and is carried by vignetted insets, summary handling, and distracting visual tricks calculated to beguile the eye of a passerby with a one-minute attention span. While the composition has an appropriate, blinking, and chaotic color dazzle like the Times Square neon and pasteboard jungle, its actual images are nostalgic references to the movie industry: a hand-cranked, primitive camera and a medallion portrait of Rudolph Valentino, among others, culled from Hollywood period photographs.

Africa II is another of the artist's paintings of monumental scale, one of those intermittent works of great scope and magnitude that have punctuated his career, bringing together in a condensed summary many of his current preoccupations of theme and presentation. Its richness and variety of surface recall the high performance level of the *Dying and Dead Veteran*. An ensemble of freely associated images from mixed sources surround the painted map of Africa, and in its layered depths the eye uncovers buried visual and social meanings. Fleeing, diminutive ghosts of camels from the cigarette pack merge with the landscape to which they also belong, connecting clashing contexts of different identity, association, and scale; a native rises majestically from the dark continent, the genie of the primitive past asserting himself in the midst of the vivid and optimistic patterns of a hybrid painting-cum-poster; a wonderfully real drawing-in-paint of a crocodile evokes the jungle swamp and thus counteracts in larger scale the camel cliché, which has been taken from standard brands rather than from the African scene. The mood of the painting combines a boyish relish for action, movement, and colorful scene with an involved and complex sense of social change.

Since *Africa II*, chromatic vivacity and painterliness have been subordinated to construction and collage, to new modes of inventiveness based on extra-pictorial means. *Dutch Masters and Cigars* reduces color to monochrome tints of gray and brown, relieved by sparse bright touches in the cigar bands. The grayed quality of the images of Rembrandt's syndics and their skeletal bareness of definition give them a relief projection; that visual illusion was then taken up quite literally in a smaller version of the same theme which was bent and shaped into actual sculptural form. Muted color, de-emphasis of handling, and repeating image groupings ranged twice in horizontal tiers accent the quality of filmic illusion. Silkscreens were used to transfer images from the first to this second, large version of *Dutch Masters and Cigars*, a device Rauschenberg and other modern disciples of news media anonymity had first utilized, but with quite a different purpose. The light-absorbing, drab brown and dun colors of the central cluster of cigars is not only descriptively accurate but literally refers to the actual color of the cardboard sheets on which the cigars are simulated. In other related work the artist peeled off the surface layer of cutout cardboard shapes, which stand out aggressively in their no-color; in the context of the whole composition they gain a mitigating felicity and read as mild color-forms as well as brute material fact.

A characteristic mixture of crude construction and fine painterly nuance was united dramatically in a painting commissioned by the Container Corporation of America on the theme of minority groups, *The Identification Manual*. This physically awkward but powerful painting brought Rivers' expressive repertory to bear on the kinds of subject matter of society that have often deeply engaged his human sympathies and artistic interests. His interpretation joined passionate identification with his subject matter and critical detachment—in this case, an ability to view reality through the eyes of the acquiescent consumer whose images are formed by the mass media. The painting is made in the form of a triptych; the left wing evokes in sketchbook rendering and grisaille an imaginary newspaper's front page with a Gothic masthead spelling out *The Blak*, glimpses of recognizable public heroes of the Negro revolution and scenes of civil disorder, punctuated by the interplay of freely written and mechanically formed letters. When closed, the same panel reveals a beautifully sustained portrait-drawing of a Negro girl, made from life. Her idealized image overlaps the adjoining large central canvas, and meets a heavy drift of black paint with an illustrated cosmetic jar and a diagonal fall of letters spelling "Dixie Peach," a reference to a preparation guaranteed to make the hair soft and manageable. Ranged in a horizontal row above are repeated female faces taken from the pages of *Ebony* in painted relief, with their ghostly inversions and fragments of printed advertising legends. It is a measure of Rivers' honesty that he feels compelled to report accurately on human vanity, regardless of color. In 1966, Rivers made a "multiple" of silkscreened and hand-drawn images and legends on Plexiglas for a CORE benefit. His candor about the commercial exploitation of the Negro by the cosmetic industry was not received with great enthusiasm.

In another line of development, Rivers' work of the early sixties revolved around two of his principal iconographic preoccupations of many years, the Nude and the Hero. In Paris in 1961 he painted the head of his second wife, Clarice, with sympathetic accuracy, labeling her features in strong block stenciled letters. He thus not only set up a contrast between fluid and mechanical draftsmanship but, on the level of information, created a personal kind of literary-visual Cubism which scrambled her features by naming them, even though the coherence of the image was not thereby destroyed. The device of itemizing with standardized mechanical letters the parts of a complete and intact human image was subsequently applied to his wife's nude figure in such paintings as *Parts of the Body: French Vocabulary Lesson III*. He repeated the theme of the nude and anatomical labels in a number of versions, large and small, with legends in a variety of foreign languages as well as in English. The explicit inventory of the body's parts creates a curious split between perception and knowledge; we see the figure as an irreplaceable human subject, individual and whole, but we are also invited to read it through a screen of word-messages as a collection of replaceable parts.

The Hero was revived in dual obsession: old master idolatry and the Napoleon image. In 1964, he painted a free copy after David's *Napoleon in His Study* in the National Gallery of Art in Washington. Napoleon's imperious pose struck Rivers suddenly as affected and mincing, and he could not resist dubbing the finished painting *The Greatest Homosexual*, which must have set some kind of a record for idiosyncrasy in deciding painting titles. The visual and mental separations by which Rivers today makes distinctions in art create a medley of disconnected old master bravura passages of a rivaling skill, and an overall effect of Madame Tussaud's waxworks. Some of the most richly inflected painting details manage to look like objects in themselves rather than pictorial metaphor or representation. Napoleon's figure is modulated from a tenuous tracing to fragments of full-blown pictorial reality. Sewn-on plastic sections, raised and attached lettering, the play of opacities and transparencies of paint surface against refined drawing leave a visible and vibrant record of image and idea in their successive stages of development, and thus they restate as the work's essential content the artist's own fantastic personal activity.

A second version, *The Second Greatest Homosexual*, startles even more with its mixed expressive modes. Twin schematic figures of Napoleon are drawn over and under layers of plastic and cardboard sheets attached to a glazed surface, or spread out as background in the interior of a large, shallow box construction. A bewitching complicity of sensuous color touches, elegant if spotty draftsmanship, and inspired woodworking produce complex impressions that confound our sense of inner and outer—x-rayed and solid—form, of transience and permanence. Fluorescent light tubes installed on the sides of the box lend the setting an air of theatrical illusion, underscoring the image's phantomlike qualities; the streaming light rays are trapped by the lucent glues that hold the plastic sheets together. The effect is one of mystery and even, at first glance, of personal myth, eccentricity, and hermeticism.

The Second Greatest Homosexual was the last construction catalogued for the large Rivers retrospective exhibition held at Brandeis University in the spring of 1965. Challenged by the prospect of having the comprehensive fifteen-year survey brought that year to the Jewish Museum in New York, Rivers set to work on an ambitious "history" painting worthy in his own mind of the commemorative occasion, and designed to give special excitement to the New York showing. During a brief bout with the flu, he had been reading Isaac Deutscher's three-volume biography of Trotsky.

6. Jacques-Louis David. *Napoleon in His Study*.
   1812. Oil on canvas, 80 1/4 × 49 1/4″.
   National Gallery of Art, Washington, D.C.
   Samuel H. Kress Collection

He began to speculate whether he might not summarize his own visual impressions of the Russian Revolution in a loose visual chronicle. The panorama of history appealed to his underlying beliefs that painting should lend itself to social issues, and man's purposes, to the traditional interests of the great art of the past in heroic action and individuals.

Further reading about the historic events of 1917 deepened his interest and commitment, and he then began to dig seriously in visual archives and to collect photographs from Sovfoto, the Soviet picture agency. Rivers planned a large work and built in his studio a rough armature of large beams and bracing planks to hold different size canvas panels and constructed elements. The work came into existence in sections as a sequence of loosely related episodes, in pencil drawing, painting, connecting sections of carpentry, and abstract sculpture. It was a combination of "narrative" painting, with vignetted episodes of the revolution, parodies of official "state" portraits of both the heroes of the revolution and the imperial court, schematic scenery, object impedimenta, written labels, and poetry. The general chronological movement of the design and main points of emphasis were established in advance, but the balance of different kinds of documentation as well as the lively alternations in a wide variety of techniques were already implicit in Rivers' current work. This monumental painting-construction, indeed, summarized brilliantly the expressive range of his style of the late fifties and early sixties.

The random assortment of images in *The Russian Revolution* follows a rough chronological order and reads from left to right. The images move from the *Communist Manifesto*, with half-erased visages of the bearded Marx and Engels, to imperial portraits of the czar and czarina, posed in stiffly brocaded magnificence; by way of dramatic contrast and relief, there is a neighboring panel with a stark, diagrammatic map showing the disastrous battlegrounds in Russia during World War I. A storm-window portrait of Lenin introduces surrounding scenes of revolution in the streets, painted over silkscreens of famous Tass photos. Storm windows and frames constructed by hand hold painted images of Trotsky, the young Stalin (ironically, in diminutive scale), and Maxim Gorky; scenes and symbols in the form of a lavish plumbing display follow, portraying the period of industrialization. Finally, at the far right, under a real pistol, the poet Mayakovsky is depicted with a painted gun at his temple, alongside a carefully hand-lettered poem which contains scornful references to politicians. The circle is complete, beginning with the association of hopeful idealism in the noble icons of Marx and Engels, and closing with the defeated idealism of the tragic poet of revolution.

When he had finished, Rivers declared that the work "must be either a masterpiece, or an absurdity." Taken in the sense of the contemporary theater, absurdity was perhaps unavoidable in encompassing a historical theme of such grandiose dimensions, whose idealistic promise political events betrayed. Absurd in a more personal sense was the effort to create a historical painting with impressionistic means more suitable for a notebook's jottings. Despite its flaws, eccentricities, and obvious technical and philosophical problems, *The Russian Revolution* did succeed miraculously in its intention. It is a work of art of extraordinary power and sustained intensity. Whether or not it is a masterpiece, only time will tell; certainly it is one of the climactic creations of the postwar period in American art. There have only been two other paintings similar in scale, encyclopedic range of imagery, and topical reference—though they are completely contemporary in content, quite unlike Rivers' nostalgic inventory of history: Rauschenberg's thirty-three-foot *Barge*, and Rosenquist's eighty-six-foot *F-111*. Both paintings mix images of action and icons of commerce and current technology in painting modes that are more smoothly integrated as physical medium. Their surfaces have a homogeneity that the Rivers' work, with its collection of disparate elements and anthology of personal styles and methods, surely lacks. For all their virtues and innovations in form and image-making, however, neither Rauschenberg's nor Rosenquist's work is more interesting dramatically as a progression of images or even more satisfying formally, within the conventions the work has erected for itself, than *The Russian Revolution*. We may deplore Rivers' old-fashioned and anachronistic means, which look technically outmoded next to the mechanically processed look of Rosenquist's blended images of action or Rauschenberg's fluent silkscreens. The power of his work lies in its unapologetic personal expressiveness, and the mixture of sophisticated means and awareness with a boyish, romantic nostalgia for heroes, action, and history. Rivers' ambitious construction represents a personal triumph and a notable exercise of the contemporary historical imagination.

Current with *The Russian Revolution* were a number of storm-window portraits done by Rivers of the artists Jim Dine and Jean Tinguely, and a commissioned portrait of a Boston businessman, Herbert Lee. The sliding glass panes, with their alternate up-down positions, gave mobility and variety to the combinations of color, shape, drawing, and shallow relief modeling. A window pane had the ambiguity of a transparent foreground and opaque background; it could be painted on or seen through. Rivers also enjoyed the cool, silver gray tone of his aluminum frames as a foil for his warm color schemes. The shocking juxtaposition of a crudely executed image in paint with efficient contemporary hardware appealed to him as well.

His sitter, Herbert Lee, was posed stiffly in a mandarinlike manner reminiscent of the frontal, iconic pose of Joseph Hirshhorn, but with a difference, since the flat, rectilinear format no longer completely contains or delimits the figure. The sitter's image changes abruptly into an environmental experience that enters into the spectator's space by means of a built-out box construction, on which his pants' folds are simultaneously modeled in paint and carved in wood. In the background are freely painted shoes, elegant female faces, hairdos, and cloche hats from the world of fashion. They are emblematic references to the occupation of the sitter, who manufactures stylish shoes for women.

The competition between an increasingly subdued pictorial illusion and emphatic construction continued in 1966 with the commercial imagery of Rivers' *Don't Fall* series, consisting of three works and a number of related, small studies. The image of a small child stepping into a bathtub, shown steeply upright in flattened perspective, was derived from a color photograph advertising the traction and the safety features of a rubber bath mat. In the largest of the constructions, the child's body is drab ocher, and the illuminated plastic letters, a displaced pink flesh tone. The large expanses of soft grays, dispersed grafitti, hammered nail holes, and indentations stand in marked contrast to the gleaming white surface of a plastic plaque with a luminous cutout legend. It is exactly the kind of juxtaposition between handmade and mechanically fabricated surfaces, between artificially bright and muted color notes, which Rivers established as favored expressive combinations in his first Pop subjects of the early sixties.

One of Rivers' most inventive and controversial works since *The Russian Revolution* was *Lampman Loves It*, a painted construction created for an erotica exhibition at the Sidney Janis Gallery. Two fantastic male and female figures are linked in the act of copulation, although their critical anatomical parts have been masked as a gooseneck lamp and a Plexiglas-enclosed cavity. The construction is made up of light boxes with superimposed color photographs, painted wood and shining plastic, found and shaped objects. Indeed, the abrupt shifts of representation, technique, and abstract structuring call attention to the artistic process so emphatically that the charade of real-life action and the sex theme are strangely eclipsed. The coupling of a mechano-man and a flat cutout in wood of a female figure lifted unceremoniously, as it seems, from a commercial signboard is less shocking than one might expect. If the work verges on bad taste because of the explicitness of the sexual theme, then its concentration on invention for its own sake and the austerities of its forms act to undercut its eroticism.

Another in a sequence of brilliant constructions was a stiffly posed family-portrait group, called *The Elimination of Nostalgia, ABC.* Based on an enlarged photograph of himself, his wife, and two sons, the figures were, in effect, fragmentary photographic icons mounted in boxlike enclosures or on shaped-canvas projections that filled them out literally as concrete forms, diffracted through the sculptural medium. There were discrete touches of modeling in paint on the eccentric-shaped canvas, with sudden points of clear vision coming into focus in facial features, wearing apparel, the shine of a boot or a glass of beer. Fantasy in color shape, the use of caricature, flat photographic image and free structural invention combined in a mad and tantalizing game which suggested Marisol's garbled identities. Yet the formal elaboration of *The Elimination of Nostalgia* is vintage and inimitable Rivers. In the matter of style, energy, or even the snapshot, instantaneous poses, it has traceable affinities with his earlier work.

Cropped Blue Bed can be linked to Rivers' recent constructions, but it is a "sport" by reason of its abstractness and parody of the shaped-canvas mode. Only Rivers could arrive at the idea for a work of art by making a monumental crumple of canvas do double duty as abstract form and the image of a young lady in bed, hugging sheets and bedspread to cover her nudity. While the manipulative potential of medium, in its current fashionable modes, was encouraged to operate freely and suggest visual content, the particular imagery that emerged was decidedly personal. What may have been sacrificed in nuanced elaboration was recovered as sculptural presence and abstract invention. There is no doubt, however, that Rivers is still capable of subtle drawing and refined attenuations of form and modeling. As evidence, there are his *Throw-away Dress: New York to Nairobi,* a virtuoso example of figure painting, and the preliminary, large colored-crayon sketches or "tryouts" for a *Boston Massacre* commissioned by a Boston bank and now completed, which revived Rivers' early American Arcadia of redcoats and colonial soldiers locked in battle and posed in period military costume. Then, recently, he brought back a sheaf of sensitive drawings and collages after an extended trip through Africa.

In the summer of 1967 he traveled through Kenya, the Congo, Nigeria, and several other African countries with the film maker Pierre Gaisseau, on assignment from NBC. An "experimental" film was commissioned by the network as a collaboration between a well-known artist and a documentary film maker of exceptional brilliance, winner of an Academy Award in 1962. Rivers had himself long been interested in film, performed as an actor in Al Leslie's *Pull My Daisy* and, in the early sixties, tried his skill at moviemaking with a hand camera at the Bronx Zoo. The Zoo was an obsession of his youth, and animal imagery returned to haunt his art on numerous occasions, of which the *Dreyfus Fund*

Lion series was the last. The point of departure for the Gaisseau-Rivers collaboration was to be Africa through the artist's eyes, through Rivers' special angle of vision. Africa held out numerous temptations; Rivers was attracted by its primitivism and exotic remoteness, combined with the social theme of emerging nations and modernization. What intrigued him especially was the effect of mass communications on the reality of Africa—the degree to which the actual experience would be insulated by the bland and unsurprising images of the picturesque which the bored and comfortable tourist carries in his own mind—images which even strange and far-off places are only meant to verify and confirm. The film venture also represented another ambitious assault on the "big" panoramic subject, like his old dream of heroes and history, topics which Hollywood hyperbole and advertising have pretty much drained of potential meaning or use for the serious artist of today. Like the Russian Revolution, Africa posed a challenge; it tickled his indefatigable curiosity about life and liberated his visual imagination, but within the framework of the untried medium of film making.

Since his African trip with Gaisseau, Rivers has been attracted obsessively to the theme of black history and, by inference, to the ordeal of a white society which may well founder on the issue and rock of racism. On the light-hearted side, there was the outrageous pun on male white supremacy which explored with relish the sexual competition implicit in that sensitive topic, entitled *America's Number One Problem*. This rather scurrilous, electrified construction offered two symmetrical profiles of the male sexual organ, one white and one black, equal in size and identical in shape, and below the provocative shapes was a depicted ruler. A scandalous subject matter combined with impersonal presentation methods has had ample precedent in Rivers' artistic past, from the nude studies of his mother-in-law to *Lampman Loves It*. He has often utilized an explicit eroticism as a screen for attacking stuffy middle-class values, but invariably his tone was ironic and the mood disinterested. He miraculously resists propagandistic effects and the temptations of audience manipulation, no matter how much he may seem to welcome a taboo subject matter bound to excite public scandal.

Rivers' boldest commentary on the black revolution grew out of a commission by the enlightened and courageous Ménil Foundation, for the Institute for the Arts at Rice University in Houston. He was invited to create an ensemble of works in the mediums and forms he preferred, summarizing or symbolizing the history and condition of the American Negro. After many months of intensive work and the expenditure of considerable energy, which involved enlisting the help of artists from the black community as well as creating his own objects, the project was completed in the spring of 1970 and then exhibited in Texas. All but seven of the forty-nine individual drawings, paintings and constructions, and *tableaux vivants* were from Rivers' own hand. They range in character from facile and innocuous pencil or painted portraits of black revolution heroes, living and dead, to gruesome lynching episodes and fantasies of slave-ship traffic to America. *I Like Olympia in Black Face* has the characteristic Rivers' reversal of role in a double image of Manet's famous composition, constructed in painted relief. Rivers' version changes the skin colors so that the maid in attendance becomes white and her mistress, black; even the Baudelairean cat emerges with an exchanged identity as a white tabby. The modes of representation include everything from the convincing replication in wood of a Harlem tenement stoop, realistically outfitted with garbage cans, to a fantastic, monumentalized plastic oxford shoe with a portrait of the inventor of the lasting machine set incongruously in the heel, rather like a commemorative medal or icon on a naive funerary monument. Six black artists collaborated with Rivers and contributed their own works to his ambitious undertaking, in what finally amounted to a loose, unstructured exhibition on the theme of black history. In an acerbic and consistently perceptive and interesting introduction to the exhibition catalogue, which was rather casually called "Some American History," the black writer Charles Childs examined Larry Rivers' ambitious project, and in so doing brought many useful insights to bear on his work as a whole:

> In tackling the vastness of black life and history . . . Larry Rivers brings to the subject his unique proximity to the black community, and his tendency to draw on the "intimacy" to make art of his own life.
>
> "Black life to me is a whole spectrum of people I've met and come to know at various times," Rivers admits. "It is a perception of race and culture with as many variables and dimensions as people are variable. Because of some of these people, I think I've become sensitized, enriched and broadened. After all," Rivers continues, "more than being an artist, I am a political man. I am affected by what other men do and say and think and what I have produced as an artist is my relationship to other men which points out our differences and our similarities."

Childs goes on:

> A roustabout hipster, Rivers gravitated to the opposite of "square" Bar-Mitzvah-type upbringing, not out of disrespect for his own Jewishness, but, here again, because of his insatiable curiosity concerning

the world around him. Like the white prototype of Norman Mailer's "white negro," Rivers paid his acculturation dues in all-night rent parties in Harlem and got his first short-sighted impressions of black life through intimate associations with pimps, street hustlers and one special whore who took him home to meet her family.

Then, in an observation that neatly capsulates Rivers' unique quality of vision, and the kind of misunderstanding it has given rise to, Childs notes:

> A compulsive urge to truth, which means truth first denied but deeply felt in spite of itself, is a recurring motif in the work of Larry Rivers. It is this successful working through to where it's really at, this victory over himself that is most corrosive. Consequently, what everybody knows as the normal and ordinary cliché, once turned upside down and laid bare by Rivers, can often prove unnerving. Perhaps this accounts for why some critics see the flamboyance of Larry Rivers as a kind of comic weakness, when actually, in a way, the free admission of his own banality, the banality epitomized in *Lamp Man Loves It*, whereby a 7-foot black man achieves vivid connection with a complacent friend by way of a flashing lightbulb, belongs to a whole area of emotional and intellectual conquests.

In his first New York gallery one-man show recently after more than five years of public inactivity on the official art scene, Rivers found himself under merciless critical attack, alternately on moral and formal grounds, either as a public scandal or for his erratic invention. His perverse celebration of the drug experience with a replica of a six-foot high heroin needle, set against a Mylar backdrop and psychedelic dream imagery, was not generally admired. Nor was the startling photographic realism of his nudity, or a new touch of morbidity in a three-dimensional version of the *Last Civil War Veteran* theme. For a middle western floral messenger service Rivers had created a schematic Union soldier shown in the exhibition standing guard over a flag-decked, floreate casket, which opened to reveal the artist's own facial mask attached to a gruesome Confederate cadaver. It was an image of surfeit worthy of Forest Lawn in its morbid luxury. At the other extreme of vivid pulsing life, he fashioned a kaleidoscopic, electrified construction swarming with athletic females in swimsuits, sprinting and whirling against a blinking environment of lipsticked mouths and elegantly sheathed body parts, entitled *Forty Feet of Fashion*. There were also constructions like *Me and My Shadow*, on the other hand, whose spontaneity and crudity recalled the rough, inspired carpentry and invention of the mixed-media works of the mid-sixties, for which *The History of the Russian Revolution* had provided an inexhaustible mine of visual ideas. While the variety of the works in Rivers' last public exhibition might open the artist to the charge of stylistic inconsistency, he had in fact remained true to his own generous and untidy talent. His wide range of subject matter, uncontained parodistic energies, and responsiveness to social issues set him apart from his contemporaries. Perhaps most significantly, he has remained faithful to his own undimmed curiosity and appetite for experience, even at the risk of banality or narcissism. He was always his own best subject matter, and that self-regarding, autobiographical obsession continues essentially unchanged.

At mid-career, Rivers has left us some of the most memorable images in paint and sculpture of a decade packed with innovation. His vision has been influential, although not necessarily decisive, in opening up to the younger genera-tion a new range of overlooked subject matter; at a critical moment in the fifties, he helped bring a fundamental change in aesthetic attitudes by offering a viable alternative to Action Painting. He still feels close to Action Painting and its ideals of personal creativity and risk, but he also has liberally appropriated to his art the mass-produced images of popular culture. Neither position defines him exhaustively nor captures the special atmosphere of his style. His own strongly accented individualism will continue, as it has in the past, to shape the powerful motives of growth, development, and fertile change in his work over the creative decades that lie before him.

Plates

7. *The Burial*. 1951. Oil on canvas, 5′ × 9′. Fort Wayne Museum of Art, Fort Wayne Art Institute, Indiana

8. Study for *Washington Crossing the Delaware* (two heads and a horse). 1953. Pencil, 11 × 13 5/8″. The Museum of Modern Art, New York

9. *Washington Crossing the Delaware.* 1953. Oil on canvas, 6'11" × 9'3". The Museum of Modern Art, New York

10. *Portrait of Berdie.* 1953.
Oil on canvas, 80 3/4 × 54 3/4".
Museum of Art, Rhode Island School of Design,
Providence

11. *Joseph.* 1954.
Oil on canvas, 52 1/2 × 45 1/2".
Collection David Daniels, New York

12. *Double Portrait of John Myers*. 1954. Bronze, height with base 72″. Collection David P. Bassine, New York

13. *Double Portrait of Berdie*. 1955. Oil on canvas, 70 3/4 × 82 1/2″.
The Whitney Museum of American Art, New York

14. *Berdie with the American Flag*. 1955. Oil on canvas, 20 × 25 7/8″. Nelson Gallery-Atkins Museum, Kansas City, Missouri. Gift of William Inge

15. *The Athlete's Dream*. 1956. Oil on canvas, 6′10″ × 9′ 10″. Marlborough-Gerson Gallery, New York

17. *The Accident*. 1957.
Oil on canvas, 84 × 90".
Collection Joseph E. Seagram & Sons, Inc.,
New York

16. *Steel Plant*. 1958. Steel, height 78".
Collection Mr. and Mrs. Thomas B. Hess, New York

18. *The Studio*. 1956.
Oil on canvas, 6′10″ × 16′1″.
The Minneapolis Institute of Arts

Second Avenue with "THE." 1958.
Oil on canvas, 72 3/4 × 82 3/4".
Collection Mr. and Mrs.
Patrick B. McGinnis, Cincinnati

20. *Drugstore.* 1959.
Oil on canvas, 85 × 66".
Marlborough-Gerson Gallery,
New York

21. *Cedar Bar Menu I*. 1959.
Oil on canvas, 47 1/2 × 35″.
Marlborough-Gerson Gallery,
New York

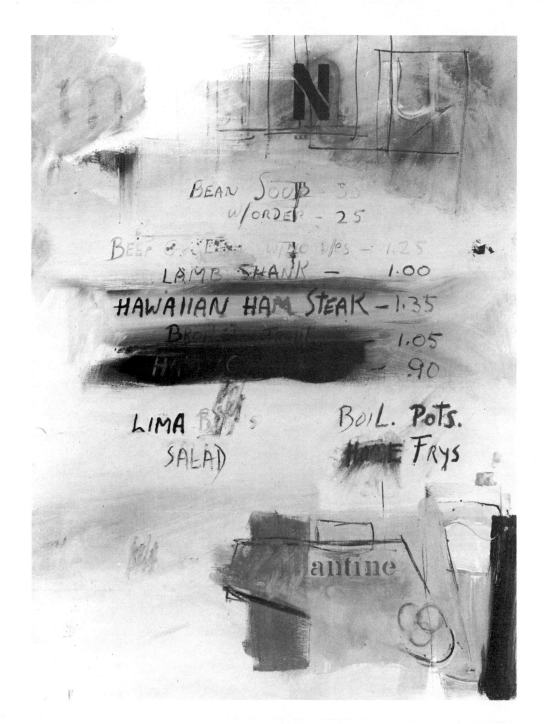

22. *Cedar Bar Menu II*. 1960.
Oil on canvas, 48 × 36″.
Collection the artist

Buick Painting with P. 1960.
Oil on canvas, 48 × 61″.
Collection Mr. and Mrs.
Richard Titelman,
Altoona, Pennsylvania

24. *Dougherty Ace of Spades.* 1960.
Oil on canvas, 74 × 56″.
Chrysler Art Museum,
Provincetown, Massachusetts

25. *Typewriter Painting I.* 1962.
Oil on canvas, 57 1/2 × 45".
Collection the artist

6. *Last Civil War Veteran*. 1961.
Oil on canvas, 82 1/2 × 64 1/2".
Collection Martha Jackson,
New York

De Kooning with My Texas Hat. 1963.
Pencil, 14 × 17″. Collection the artist

28. *Portrait of Joseph H. Hirshhorn*. 1963.
Oil on canvas, 71 × 48″.
Joseph H. Hirshhorn Collection

29. *French Money I.* 1961. Oil on canvas, 35 1/4 × 59″. Marlborough-Gerson Gallery, New York

30. *Camels, 6 by 4.* 1962.
Oil on canvas, 72 × 48″.
Collection Mrs. J. Frederick Byers III,
New York

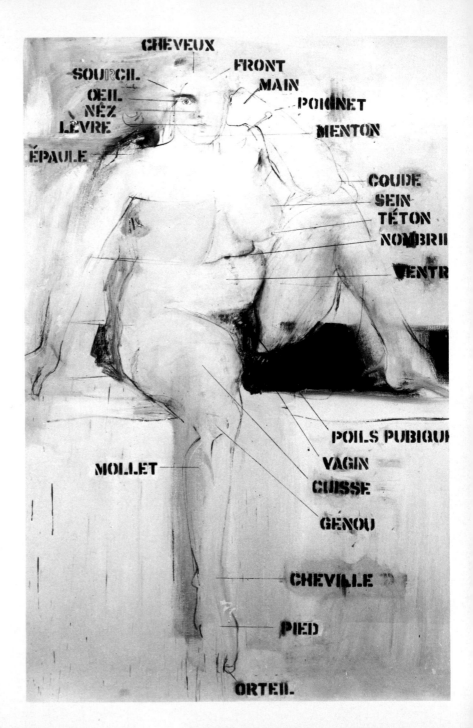

31. *Parts of the Body: French Vocabulary Lesson III.*
1962. Oil on canvas, 72 × 48″.
Collection Mr. and Mrs. Robert C. Scull,
New York

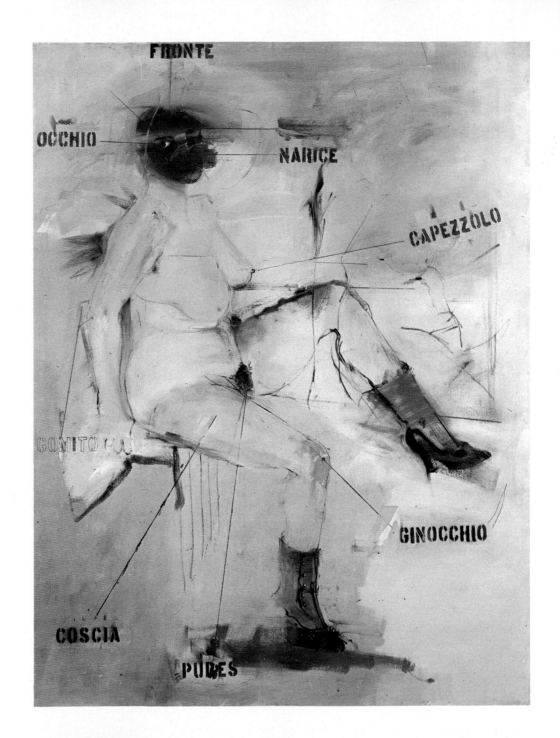

FRONTE

OCCHIO

NARICE

CAPEZZOLO

GOMITO

GINOCCHIO

COSCIA

PUBES

32. *Parts of the Body:
Italian Vocabulary Lesson.*
1963. Oil on canvas, 69 × 52″.
Marlborough-Gerson Gallery,
New York

33. *First New York Film Festival Billboard.* 1963. Oil on canvas, 9′ 6″ × 15′. Joseph H. Hirshhorn Foundation

34. *Dutch Masters and Cigars.*
1963. Oil and board collage
on canvas, 96 × 67 3/8″.
The Harry N. Abrams Family
Collection, New York

. *Africa II*. 1963.
Oil on canvas, 9'4" × 11'1".
Collection Mr. and Mrs. Robert Mnuchin,
New York

36. *Window Webster*. 1963.
Collage on board, 60 × 40".
Marlborough-Gerson Gallery, New York

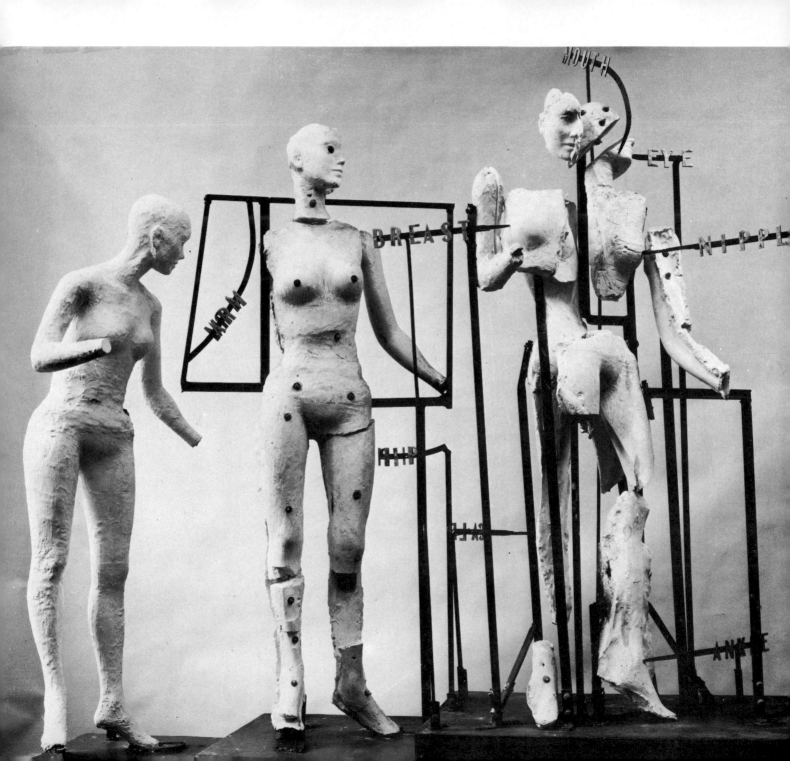

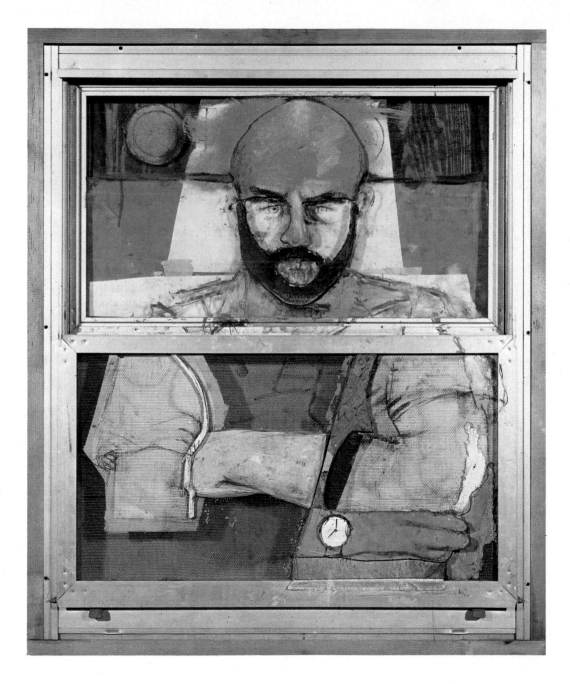

Parts of the Body:
English Vocabulary Lesson.
1964. Plaster and steel,
83 3/4 × 90 1/2 × 24 1/4″.
Collection the artist

38. *Jim Dine Storm Window.*
1965. Mixed media,
29 × 25 × 2 3/4″.
Collection the artist

39. *The Identification Manual* (open). 1964. Oil and collage on canvas; left panel, 32 × 25″; center panel, 72 × 52″; right panel, 47 × 30″. Collection Container Corporation of America

40. *Webster and Cigars.* 1966. Mixed media collage on wood construction, 13 1/4 × 16 × 13 1/4″. Collection the artist

41. *The History of the Russian Revolution: From Marx to Mayakovsky*. 1965. Mixed media construction, 14′4″ × 32′5″ × 1
Joseph H. Hirshhorn Foundation

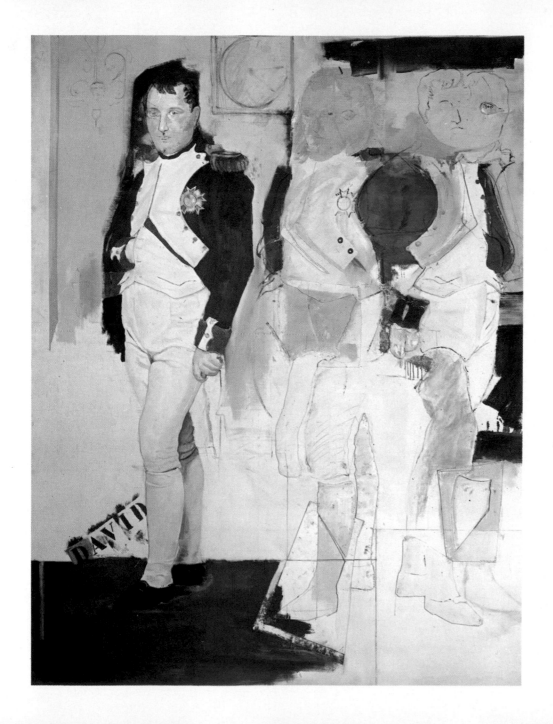

42. *The Greatest Homosexual.* 1964.
Oil and collage on canvas, 80 ×
Joseph H. Hirshhorn Collection

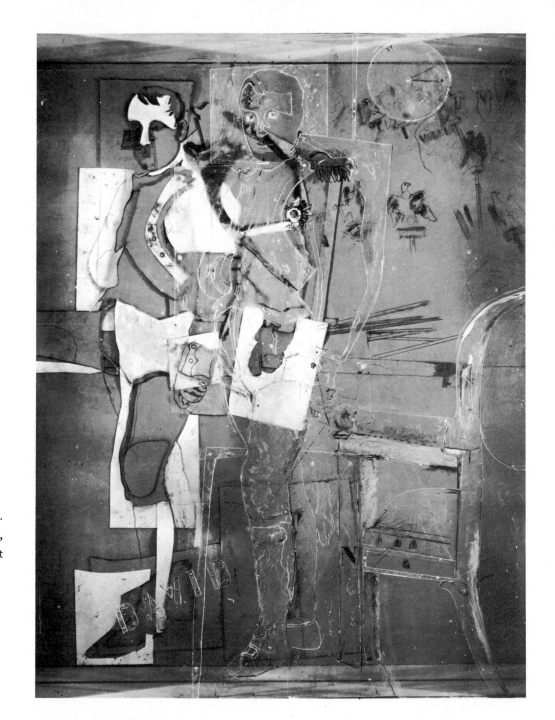

The Second Greatest Homosexual. 1965.
xiglas, collage, electric light and wood,
74 1/2 × 62 1/2″. Collection the artist

44. *Don't Fall.* 1966.
Oil, plastic, metal with neon light, height 94″.
Collection the artist

45. *Lampman Loves It*. 1966.
Sculpture, with Plexiglas, painted wood, and light,
8'10" × 65" × 29". Collection the artist

46. *The Elimination of Nostalgia, ABC.*
1967. Mixed media,
84 × 64 1/2 × 25 3/4″.
Holzer Collection, New York

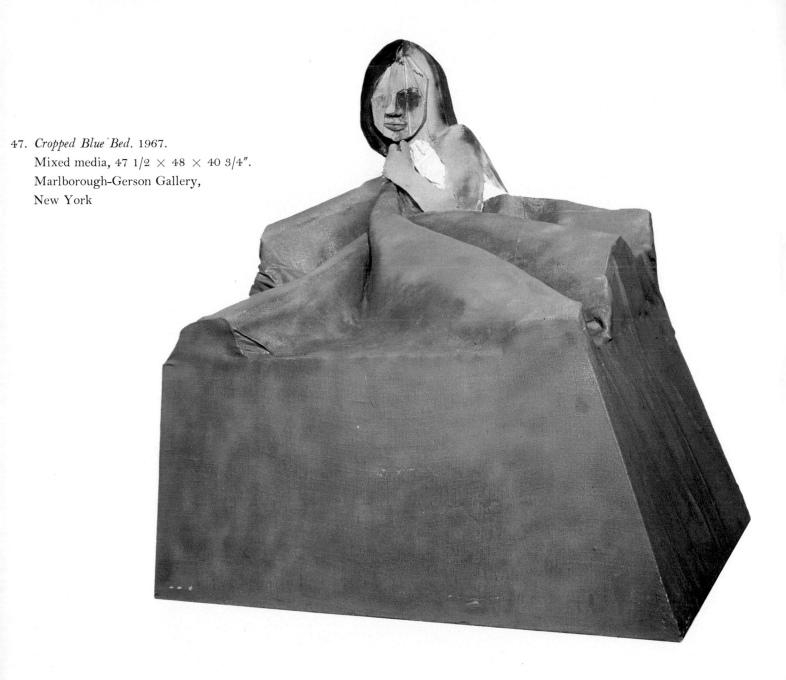

47. *Cropped Blue Bed.* 1967.
   Mixed media, 47 1/2 × 48 × 40 3/4″.
   Marlborough-Gerson Gallery,
   New York

48. *Untitled* (African girl
with lion in stencil).
1968. Collage, 24 × 18".
Collection the artist

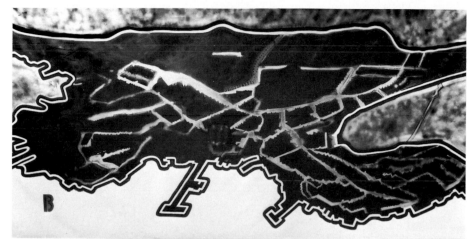

49. *The Boston Massacre* (unfinished).
1968. Acrylic and oil on canvas, 19′6″ × 14′.
Collection The New England Merchants
National Bank of Boston

The Paul Revere Event—Four Views (detail)
1968. Acrylic and oil on canvas.
Collection The New England Merchants
National Bank of Boston

51. *Bad Witch*. 1970.
Mixed media, 90 × 64″.
Marlborough-Gerson Gallery, New York

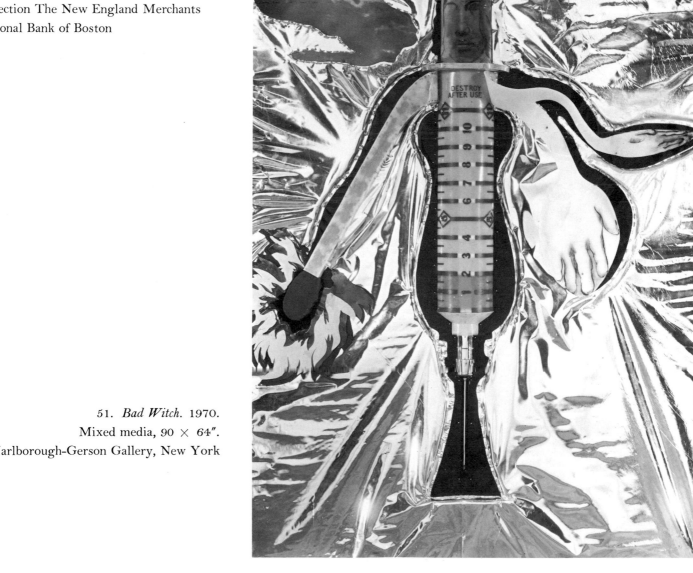

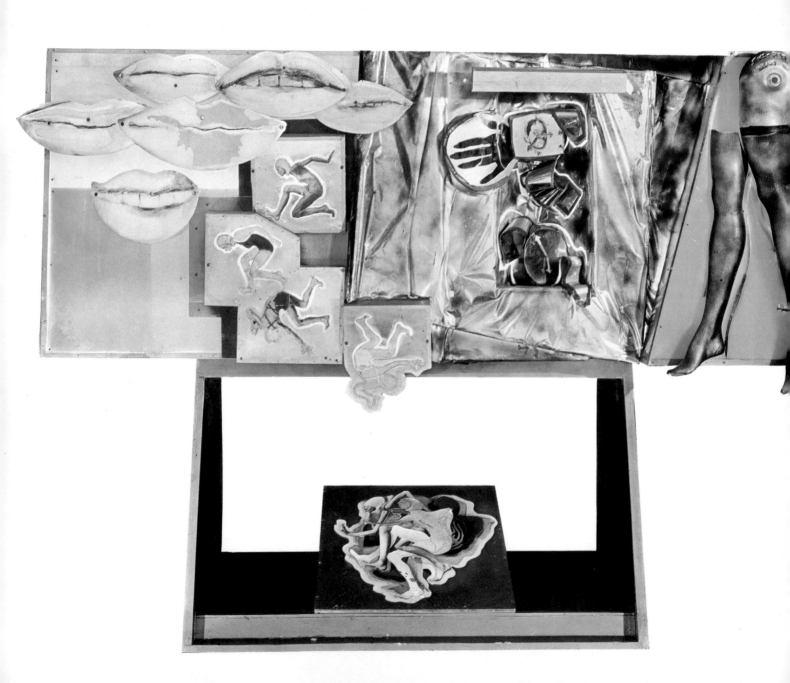

Forty Feet of Fashion. 1970.
Plexiglas mixed media,
$74 \times 97 \times 30''$.
Collection the artist

3. *Caucasian Woman Sprawled
on a Bed and Figures
of Hanged Men.*
1970. Construction.
Ménil Foundation, Houston

54. *I Like Olympia in Black Face*. 1970. Mixed media construction, 41 × 78 × 34″.
Ménil Foundation, Houston

55. Foreground: *A Slave Ship*. 1970. Construction, 13′6″ × 22′ × 4′6″
Background: *The Ghetto Stoop*. 1969. Construction, 13′6″ × 10′4″ × 8′10″
Ménil Foundation, Houston

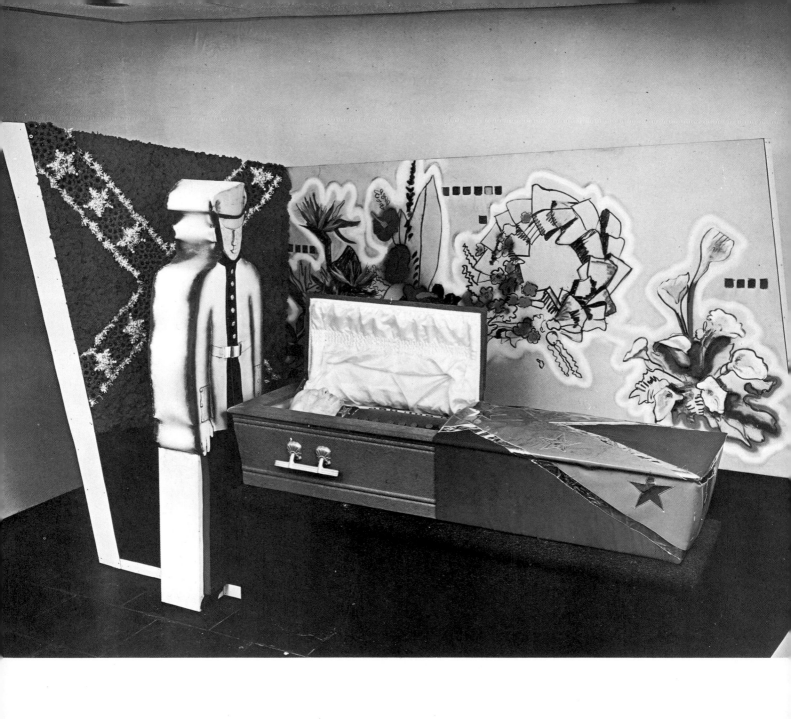

Biography

Born August 17 in the Bronx, New York, the only son and eldest child of Samuel and Sonya Grossberg. Father was a plumber, and later owned a small trucking company.

1940 Began musical career as a jazz saxophonist.

1942 Enlisted in the United States Army Air Corps.

1943 Received a medical discharge from the armed forces.

1944 Studied composition at the Juilliard School of Music, New York, for a year. 1943–45, played saxophone in jazz bands in and around New York with Shep Fields, Jerry Wald, and Johnny Morris, among others.

1945 Started painting during the summer at Old Orchard Beach, Maine, with Jane Freilicher, while playing in a band with her husband. Married Augusta Burger.

1946 Separated from Augusta and moved to an apartment in Manhattan near the painter Nell Blaine, the first established New York avant-garde artist he met.

1947 Attended Hans Hofmann's school of painting from January, 1947 through the summer of 1948, in New York and Provincetown.

1948 Began studying art at New York University with the objective of supporting himself by

6. *Last Civil War Veteran*. 1970.
Mixed media construction, 7′ × 10′3″ × 3′6″.
From "Each in His Own Way,"
the Commemorative Art Collection of the Florists'
Transworld Delivery Association

teaching painting. William Baziotes was one of his teachers. Became interested in Bonnard after viewing large exhibition of his painting at the Museum of Modern Art. Met Willem de Kooning, Edwin Denby, Rudolph Burckhardt, and Kenneth Koch at this time.

1949   First one-man exhibition at the Jane Street Gallery, New York.

1950   First trip to Europe; visited France and Italy. Spent eight months in Paris painting and writing. Upon his return to New York, met many of the most important artists of the American vanguard, including Franz Kline and Philip Guston; also began to see younger artists, Grace Hartigan, Alfred Leslie, and Helen Frankenthaler, and the dealer John Myers. Met poets Frank O'Hara and John Ashbery. Mother-in-law, Bertha "Berdie" Burger, and Rivers' two sons, Joseph and Steven, shared household; Berdie's financial assistance permitted him to devote himself exclusively to painting.

1951   Met Jackson Pollock. Completed first major work, *The Burial*, inspired by Gustave Courbet's *A Burial at Ornans*. John Myers' Tibor de Nagy Gallery, New York, became his representative. Held first one-man exhibition there in December. Began to make plaster sculpture. Graduated from New York University, and began to spend summers in Southampton, Long Island.

1952   Designed sets for the play, *Try! Try!*, by Frank O'Hara, directed by Herbert Machiz, produced for the Artists' Theater by John Myers.

1953   Spent part of the winter as well as summer in Southampton and completed *Washington Cross-*

ing the Delaware (acquired by the Museum of Modern Art, New York, in 1955).

1954   Gloria Vanderbilt foundation acquired *The Burial*, on the advice of Meyer Schapiro, acting as consultant; the painting was later given to the Fort Wayne Art School and Museum, Fort Wayne, Indiana.

1955   Awarded third prize, The 24th Biennial Exhibition of Contemporary Oil Paintings, Corcoran Gallery of Art, Washington, D.C., for *Self-Figure*, acquired by the Corcoran Gallery.

1957   Began working in welded metal sculpture. Collaborated with Frank O'Hara on twelve lithographs combining illustration and poetry. This portfolio, *Stones*, was completed and printed in 1959. Berdie Burger died on Labor Day, age 66.

1958   Stayed in Paris for a month and played there in several jazz bands.

1960   Began collaboration with poet Kenneth Koch on painting-poems, *New York, 1950–60*, *Post Cards*, and others.

1961   Married Clarice Price, a Welsh-born teacher of music and art, in London. Stayed in Paris in a studio adjacent to Jean Tinguely's in the Impasse Ronsin; painted there from October to July, 1962.

1964   Trip to London, where he was given a studio at the Slade School of Fine Arts, University of London, January through June. Met regularly with students; traveled through France, Spain, and Morocco. Returned to New York and Southampton in June. Designed sets for two one-act plays, *The Toilet* and *The Slave*, by Le Roi Jones, at the St. Mark's Playhouse, New York. A daughter Gwynne was born September 10.

1965 Comprehensive retrospective exhibition organized in April at Rose Art Museum, Brandeis University, with 170 paintings, sculptures, drawings, and prints. The exhibition subsequently toured the Jewish Museum, New York, Pasadena Museum of Art, and the Minneapolis Institute of Arts.

Worked six months on giant construction-painting thirty-three feet in breadth, *History of the Russian Revolution: From Marx to Mayakovsky*, shown during his exhibition at Manhattan's Jewish Museum, and then exhibited once again in January, 1966 at the same museum.

1966 At work on *Don't Fall* and other construction-painting series.

June: designed sets and costumes on commission from Conductor Lukas Foss for Stravinsky's *Oedipus Rex*, performed at Lincoln Center, New York.

Death of Frank O'Hara, July, from injuries sustained in Fire Island jeep accident.

August 10, birth of daughter Emma in Southampton.

Winter of 1966–67 spent in London, sharing house with Howard and Mary Kanovitz, and working on large color lithograph with cutouts and collage: *Robert Fraser's London*. Produced by Christopher Prater.

1967 First African trip to make collaborative film for television with Pierre Gaisseau, through Kenya, Nigeria, the Congo, Ethiopia, Rwanda, Tanzania, and other countries. Film, tentatively entitled *Africa and I*, was commissioned by the National Broadcasting Corporation. (In 1962, Gaisseau's film documentary about New Guinea, *The Sky Above—the Mud Below*, won an Academy Award.)

Exhibition at the Museum of Modern Art, New York, of memorabilia and lithographs by Rivers and other artists for Frank O'Hara memorial volume, *In Memory of My Feelings*, produced for the Museum by Grafton Graphic, New York.

1968 Second trip to Africa with Pierre Gaisseau to complete experimental television film.

January 8: Rivers and Gaisseau narrowly escaped death in Lagos, Nigeria, when an army major ordered them executed on suspicion that they were white mercenaries fighting in the Nigerian civil war. Imprisoned and then released, after execution order was withdrawn; returned to New York to edit and process African film.

Completed monumental pair of mural canvases, over nineteen feet in height, for the New England Merchants National Bank of Boston on the theme of the Boston Massacre.

1969 Completed commission for Smithhaven Mall, *Forty Feet of Fashion*.

1970 Finished work on *Objects of American History*.

Lives and works in New York City and Southampton, Long Island.

List of Exhibitions

National Gallery of Art, Washington, D.C.
"Paintings from the Museum of Modern Art, New York," 1964
The New School Art Center, New School for Social Research, New York
"Portraits from the American Art World," 1965
"Inaugural Exhibition," 1969
Rose Art Museum, Brandeis University, Waltham, Massachusetts
"American Art Since 1950," 1962
"Brandeis University Recent Acquisitions: The Gevirtz-Mnuchin Collection and Related Gifts," 1963 (shown also at the Samuel M. Kootz Gallery, New York)
"Recent American Drawings," 1964
"Larry Rivers," retrospective exhibition, 1965 (circulated with additions to Jewish Museum, New York; The Pasadena Art Museum, Pasadena, California; and the Minneapolis Institute of Arts, Minneapolis, Minnesota)
Seattle World's Fair, Seattle, Washington
"Art Since 1950," 1962
The Stable Gallery, New York
"Sculpture by Larry Rivers," 1954 (one-man show)
Tibor de Nagy Gallery, New York
Successive one man shows every year, except 1955, from 1951 through 1962
University Art Gallery, University of New Mexico, Albuquerque
"The Painter and the Photograph," 1964
Virginia Museum, Richmond
"American Painting 1970," 1970
Whitney Museum of American Art, New York
"Art of the U.S.," 1966

Worcester Art Museum, Worcester, Massachusetts
"The New American Realism," 1965

FOREIGN EXHIBITIONS

The Hague, The Netherlands
Gemeentemuseum
"New Realism," 1964
Kassel, Germany
Museum Fridericianum
"Documenta III," 1964
"Documenta IV," 1968
Lausanne, Switzerland
Musée Cantonal des Beaux-Arts
"Premier Salon International des Galeries Pilotes, Lausanne—Artistes et Découvreurs de Notre Temps," 1963
London, England
The Tate Gallery
"Painting and Sculpture of a Decade, 1954–1964" (organized by Calouste Gulbenkian Foundation, 1964)
Gimpel Fils Gallery
"Rivers," 1962
"Larry Rivers," 1964
São Paulo, Brazil
Museu de Arte Moderna
"IV Bienal Do Museu de Arte Moderna de São Paulo," 1957
Spoleto, Italy
Festival of Two Worlds
"Disegni Americani Moderni," 1961 (assembled and circulated throughout Europe by the Museum of Modern Art, New York)

Bibliography

BOOKS

Soby, James Thrall, *Modern Art and the New Past* (Norman, Oklahoma: University of Oklahoma Press, 1958), pp. 192–196.

Grohmann, Will, ed., *Art Since 1945* (New York: Harry N. Abrams, Inc., 1958), pp. 283–331. "USA," by Sam Hunter.

Friedman, B. H., ed., *School of New York: Some Younger Artists* (New York: Grove Press, Inc., 1959), pp. 60–65. "Larry Rivers: the Next to Last Confederate Soldier," by Frank O'Hara.

Rodman, Selden, ed., *Conversations with Artists* (New York: Capricorn Books, 1961), pp. 115–121.

Nordness, Lee, and Weller, Allen S., *Art: U.S.A.: Now* (New York: Viking Press, 1963), pp. 404–407.

Rosenberg, Harold, *The Anxious Object; Art Today and Its Audience* (New York: The Horizon Press, 1964), pp. 64, 85, 238.

New Art Around the World (New York: Harry N. Abrams, Inc., 1966), pp. 9–58. "American Art Since 1945," by Sam Hunter.

EXHIBITION CATALOGUES

Twenty-fourth Biennial Exhibition of Contemporary American Oil Paintings. Washington, D.C.: Corcoran Gallery of Art, 1955.

Recent Drawings U.S.A. New York: Museum of Modern Art, Museum of Modern Art Bulletin, 23:4, 1956.

12 Americans (ed., Dorothy C. Miller; texts by the artists and others). New York: Museum of Modern Art, 1956.

Twenty-fifth Biennial Exhibition of Contemporary American Oil Paintings. Washington, D.C.: Corcoran Gallery of Art, 1957.

Rivers: Recent Paintings, Prints and Sculptures. New York: Tibor de Nagy Gallery, 1958.

Contemporary American Painting and Sculpture. Urbana: University of Illinois, 1959.

The Aldrich Collection. New York: American Federation of Arts, 1960.

Paintings, Drawings and Sculpture from the Collection of Mr. and Mrs. Patrick B. McGinnis. Lincoln, Massachusetts: De Cordova and Dana Museum and Park, 1960.

Larry Rivers. New York: Tibor de Nagy Gallery, 1960.

Pittsburgh International Exhibition of Contemporary Painting and Sculpture. Pittsburgh: Carnegie Institute, Department of Fine Arts, 1961.

Sixty-fourth American Exhibition: Paintings, Sculpture. Chicago: Art Institute of Chicago, 1961.

Art Since 1950, American: Seattle World's Fair (text by Sam Hunter). Seattle, 1962. (Separate catalogue, Rose Art Museum, Brandeis University, Waltham, Massachusetts.)

Recent Painting U.S.A.: The Figure. New York: Museum of Modern Art, 1962.

Rivers (texts by John Ashbery and Thomas B. Hess). London: Gimpel Fils Gallery, 1962.

Sixty-fifth Annual American Exhibition: Some Directions in Contemporary Painting and Sculpture (foreword by A. James Speyer). Chicago: Art Institute of Chicago, 1962.

Brandeis University Recent Acquisitions: the Gevirtz-Mnuchin Collection and Related Gifts (text by Sam Hunter). New York: Kootz Gallery, and Waltham: Rose Art Museum, Brandeis University, 1963.

Contemporary American Painting and Sculpture. Urbana: Krannert Art Museum, University of Illinois, 1963.

Le Salon International des Galeries Pilotes Lausanne—Artistes et Découvreurs de Notre Temps. Lausanne: Musée Cantonal des Beaux-Arts, 1963.

Paintings from the Museum of Modern Art, New York. Washington, D.C.: National Gallery of Art, 1963.

Painting and Sculpture of a Decade, 1954–1964. London: Tate Gallery, 1964.

Documenta III. Kassel: Museum Fridericianum, 1964.

Pittsburgh International Exhibition of Contemporary Painting and Sculpture. Pittsburgh: Carnegie Institute, Department of Fine Arts, 1964.

Larry Rivers (introduction by Larry Rivers). London: Gimpel Fils Gallery, 1964.

Recent American Drawings (foreword by Sam Hunter; introduction by Thomas H. Garver). Waltham: Rose Art Museum, Brandeis University, 1964.

The Painter and the Photograph (text by Van Deren Coke). Albuquerque: University of New Mexico Art Gallery, 1964.

Larry Rivers (text by Sam Hunter, with a statement by the artist, and "A Memoir," by Frank O'Hara). Waltham: Rose Art Museum, Brandeis University, 1965.

Larry Rivers: Drawings 1949–1969 (introduction by Carol O. Selle). Chicago: Art Institute of Chicago, 1970.

Some American History (introduction by Charles Childs). Houston: Institute for the Arts, Rice University, 1971.

PERIODICALS

Apollo

75:24 (July, 1961). "Worsdell, Waters and Rivers at Woodstock Gallery," by J. Reichardt.

75:197 (December, 1961). "Flats, Shoes, Buicks, and Websters: Exhibition in New York," by M. L. D. Mastai.

76:302 (June, 1962). Review exhibition, "Exhibition in London," Gimpel Fils Gallery, London.

79:426 (May, 1964). "Exhibition at Gimpel Fils," by J. Burr.

Art Digest

27:18 (December 15, 1952). Review exhibition at Tibor de Nagy Gallery.

28:17 (January 1, 1954). Review exhibitions at Tibor de Nagy Gallery and at Stable Gallery.

28:15–16 (January 15, 1954). "Symposium: The Creative Process."

Art in America

46:24–26 (Winter, 1958–1959). "Painting—Problems of Portraiture," by Dorothy G. Seckler.

51:125 (April, 1963). "New Venture—The Hilton Hotel Collection," by Cleve Gray.

51:134 (June, 1963). "New York's Season's Gleanings," by Hilton Kramer.

51:28–33 (December, 1963). "Artist in America: Victim of the Culture Boom?," by Dorothy G. Seckler.

52:22 (August, 1964). "Fifty-six Painters and Sculptors."

53:83 (December, 1965). "Tatyana Grosman's Workshop," by C. Gray.

55:46 (January, 1967). "Sensibility of the Sixties," by Larry Rivers.

Art International

V/1:34–35 (February 1, 1961). "New York Letter," by Irving H. Sandler.

V/2:36–39 (March 1, 1961). "Larry Rivers," by Nicolas Calas.

VI/1:71 (February, 1962). "New York Notes," by Max Kozloff.

VI/3:61 (April, 1962). "Paris Letter," by John Ashbery.

VII/1:77–78 (January 25, 1963). "New York Letter," by Sonya Rudikoff.

VII/6:79–80 (June 25, 1963), "Los Angeles Letter," by Jules Langsner.

X/9:17–25 (November, 1966), "Larry Rivers," by Sydney Simon.

Art News

48:47 (April, 1949). Review exhibition at Jane Street Gallery.

52:56–59 (January, 1954). "Rivers Paints a Picture: Portrait of Berdie," by Fairfield Porter.

52:66 (January, 1954). Review exhibition at Stable Gallery.

53:26–27 (January, 1955). "Young Draftsman on Master Draftsmen," by Larry Rivers.

55:9 (December, 1956). Review exhibition at Tibor de Nagy Gallery.

56:40–43 (March, 1957). "Purple-patch of Fetichism," by Parker Tyler.

56:11 (December, 1957). Review exhibition at Tibor de Nagy Gallery.

57:14 (December, 1958). Review exhibition at Tibor de Nagy Gallery.

59:27–28 (April, 1960). "Monet: The Eye is Magic," by Larry Rivers.

59:38 (December, 1960). "Two Sculptors, Two Painters for December."

60:44–46 (March, 1961). "Discussion of the Work of Larry Rivers," by Larry Rivers.

60:11 (December, 1961). Review exhibition at Tibor de Nagy Gallery.

60:37 (January, 1962). "Is there an American Print Revival?," by James Schuyler.

61:13 (December, 1962). Review exhibition at Tibor de Nagy Gallery.

64:35–37+(April, 1965). "Rivers' Commedia dell'arte," by Harold Rosenberg.

64:36–37+(October, 1965). "Larry Rivers' History of the Russian Revolution: retrospective at the Jewish Museum," by T. B. Hess.

65:32–33+(February, 1967). "Blues for Yves Klein," by Larry Rivers.

66:31 (April, 1967). "Jackson Pollock: An Artists' Symposium," by Larry Rivers.

Arts

30:48 (January, 1956). "Month in Review: Contemporary Group of New York Painters at Stable Gallery," by Leo Steinberg.

33:60 (December, 1958). Review exhibition at Tibor de Nagy Gallery.

33:49 (June, 1959). Review exhibition, "Recent Sculpture, U.S.A.," Museum of Modern Art, by Hilton Kramer.

36:41 (February, 1962). "Exhibition at de Nagy Gallery," by Sidney Tillim.

40:49–52 (November, 1965). "Sculpture of Larry Rivers," by William Berkson.

40:7 (December, 1965). Correction.

Arts Digest

29:22 (December 15, 1954). Review exhibition at Tibor de Nagy Gallery.

Burlington Magazine

103:36 (January, 1961). "Abstract-symbolical Paint-ings at the Tibor de Nagy Gallery," by Stuart Preston.

104:314 (July, 1962). "Americans Exhibiting in London," by A. Brookner.

Canadian Art

23:41 (January, 1966). "Destruction: A Factor in Contemporary Art," by E. H. Turner.

Commonweal

84:400 (June 24, 1966). "Rivers: Boy Painter," by B. Kaufman.

Esquire

62:43 (January, 1965). "The Art Establishment," by Harold Rosenberg.

Evergreen Review

5:19 (July-August, 1961). "How to Proceed in the Arts," by Larry Rivers and Frank O'Hara (written in 1954).

Horizon

V/2:1 (September-October, 1959). "Why I Paint As I Do," an interview by Frank O'Hara.

Journal of Aesthetics and Art Criticism

4:552 (Summer, 1966). "Dada, Camp and the Mode Called Pop," by J. A. Richardson.

Life

45:100–101 (October 20, 1958). "Wonder Boy and His Many Sides."

Location

1:1 (Spring, 1963). "My Life among the Stones," by Larry Rivers.

Locus Solus

1:3–4 (Winter, 1962). Six poems by Larry Rivers (written in 1954).

Look

31: regional editions following p. 80 (March 21, 1967). "Larry Rivers' Living Room," by M. Simons.

Mademoiselle

53:252–253 (August, 1961). "We Hitch Our Wagons to a Star," an interview with Larry Rivers.

The Nation

168:453–454 (April 26, 1949). Review of exhibition at Jane Street Gallery, by Clement Greenberg.

173:313–314 (October 13, 1951). Review exhibition at Tibor de Nagy Gallery, by Manny Farber.

186:59–60 (January 18, 1958). Review exhibition at Tibor de Nagy Gallery, by Maurice Grosser.

193:519–520 (December 23, 1961). Review exhibition at Tibor de Nagy Gallery, by Max Kozloff.

New Statesman

67:739 (May 8, 1964). "Voyeurs," by N. Lynton.

Newsweek

60:92 (December 17, 1962). Review exhibition at Tibor de Nagy Gallery.

62:75 (September 2, 1963). "Street Scene."

65:54–59 (January 4, 1965). "Vanity Fair: the New York Art Scene."

65:86 (April 26, 1965). "Jam Session."

New Yorker

37:62 (December 23, 1961). "Art Galleries: New Paintings at Tibor de Nagy Gallery," by Robert M. Coates.

New York Times

Magazine: 34–35, 78–83 (February 13, 1966). "Rivers Paints Himself into the Canvas," by Grace Glueck.

Drama section: 3 (February 5, 1967). "What is Pinter up to?" Statement by Larry Rivers, "Begin Anywhere."

Quadrum

14:120–121 (1963). "New York Letter," by Irving H. Sandler.

18:99–114, 183–184 (1965). "Larry Rivers," by S. Hunter.

Saturday Review

38:23–24 (September 3, 1955). "An Interview with Larry Rivers," by James Thrall Soby.

Seventeen

23:11 (November, 1964). "Dear Teen-age Audience," by Larry Rivers.

Studio

1964:75 (August, 1962). "You Can't Write Off the British: London Commentary," by G. S. Whittet.

Time

76:70 (December 19, 1960). Review exhibition at Tibor de Nagy Gallery.

85:94–95 (April 16, 1965). "Quipster."